IN SEARCH OF HUMANITY

S. BLESSY EVANGELINE

Made with ♥ on the Notion Press Platform
www.notionpress.com

Contents

Preface

Life span of human being is more precious to observe. World is full of living things with six sense compare with living creature of five sense (For ex: Animals, birds, plants). The little of the Book "In Search of Humanity" is very complicated to understand by analysing each one of an individual soul. Humanity must be, should be, will be in Human creature only, but there is vast lack of humanity in Human. The way to accept and recognise the qualities of human is by the Fruit of Spirit. According to catechism, the Fruit of Spirit are Love, joy, peace, patience, kindness generosity, faithfulness, gentleness, self-control follow in the life.

This book was divided into three parts: Poem, Little thought to live and Quotes about the major concept of humanity. I believe that the word, line, stanza, sentence of this book will speak to your heart. We are precious and treasures to get the countless blessings from God for being a human in this world. So, let's all live a life with good qualities and try to prove that we've human with the characteristics of Fruit of Spirit.

Acknowledgements

First of all, I thank the Almighty for his protection and grace on me. And I convey my foremost gratefulness to my excellent Motivator Mrs. C. Thenmozhi, M.A., M.Phil., (Assistant professor & Assistant controller of Examination) in Government college for Women (Autonomous), Kumbakonam. I thank Ms. S. Kiruthika M.A., (Soft skills trainer) in Mass Educational and charitable trust, Kumbakonam. She was a personal editor of my writings and she was so passionate to hear my writings then and there. At last, I'm grateful to my parents, family members and friends for their kind help and cooperation.

About Us

Kashish Publications is a growing platform for all budding writers to fulfill their dream. It is founded by Kashish Soni, a budding writer who believes that writing is the magic to heal one's heart.

"*YOU DREAM, WE ACCOMPLISHED!*"

You can contact us for solo publishing or for compiling one of our own.

Instagram id- @kashish_publications
Gmail- sonikashish004@gmail.com

About The Author

Blessy Evangeline was born and brought up in Tamil Nadu.She is fond of reading and writing poetry. She was inspired to become a writer after understanding the creations and creatures created by God. That understanding came to her from analysing lot of famous novelists, poets in English Literature who have seen simple things in different aspect. She started writing at the age of fourteen. As she grew older, she progressed to write more poems, Quotes and articles. She had been taken part as co-author for more than fifteen books. She took keen interest in search of humanity in human. Her writing is based on the theme of kindling the heart of readers to be strong in realistic life neither than on imagery. Her motive is to reach every readers through her smart and simple way of words.

1
POEMS

RELAXATION

Remember to pick up the essential

Recall the matters to pursue

Recreate your ideas to reveal

Refuse to do evil activities

Regret about the things that you have mistaken

Relax to release your burden

During the peace circumstances

Among the ministers of good things (stars)

And majesty of good deeds (moon).

Repeat re-repeat this in reality.

HOUR WITH YOUR HEART

Set aside your free time four heart

Then heart will also feel free

Because, it's your/our producerIn the busy as a bee world,

People are running after their goal

Not only too achieve

But also to fill their stomach.

To notice, some people didn't analyse to where they run.

Earth is unstable

But, heart is stable until our death.

Don't be tensed of this unstable

Give a second, minute, hour to your heart.

It teaches you to be "you"

And not to be like others.

Speak to your heart

It will speak to you.

THE REAL CONFESSION

One morning she was called

By her mom for help.

I was busy with my work, she told.

After a hour she came down

To do her work done.

Her mom was waiting for her presence.

She was busy with asking what to do.

Mom replied that to comb her hair once.

She wrought her work what she needs to do,

Bid a goodbye with busy voice.

In the eventide, when she return

She saw her mom entering into the car

With her sister in(side).

This is the last scene of seeing her (mom)

Alive in her life.

Her mom was admitted in hospital
As usual due to her excess of diabetics.
But, she stayed home with her mates.
At midnight she receives a call.

A call of bitter news
About the loser soul
Of her mom from the earth
Peeled her memories to feel
Of lost time without mom
Instead, she was only busy with works.

She regrets for spending time
Only for herself, not for mom.
She realized that boasting herself
With the word “busy”
And keeping busy in vain.

Spend, share, schedule your time

For your parents, siblings

Lest of regretting after losing.

Have an equal balance with your 's.

Bid farewell to "regret".

A JOURNEY TOWARDS NATURE

Natures nurtures everyone

To inhale the oxygen.

Nature lovers has separate

Nobility to care the creation

Gifted by God

When people hate by harsh words.

The human soul will search for loneliness

Especially lonely with nature

Refreshes the mind by the creature

Bestowed by Almighty.

Plants with polychromatic flowers

Peels the better memories,

Pastes the careful thought

In every heart of human creature

Prized by the Lord.

Herbs with multi variety

Heals the queasy body,

Helps the man to take medicine

From the natural scene

Rewarded by the Majesty.

Trees with lots of branches

Traps the sunlight which reflects

Towards the living creature

In the fertile land

Created by the Son of God.

Forest with dense trees

Flings moisturised breeze

For the weary soul

Blow by the wind mill

Blessed by the Holy Ghost.

Journey to each step of nature

Jiggle about the God's grandeur,

Judge the humankind

To give birth to nature

Mapped by the Magnifier.

Only saving trees isn't important

Oath to planting is also necessary,

Obviously, nature is our companion

To every broken heart

Donated by the omnipotent.

UPRIGHT

Wherever I go it comes with me.

Wherever I go I see it.

Wherever I stand it stands with me.

Wherever I speak it overhears me.

But, one day I upright my head

With lots of voice playing in my mind

That is the voice of human around me.

I seen its beauty under the shapeless cloud.

The most inspiring is the band of colour (rainbow).

A prism informs me the possibility

To live a life with colourful thoughts.

I reached the sky only with an emotional touch.

I have experienced and experiencing.

Now I induce you to upright your head,

What I have looked. 'It' is the sky.

LIGHT HOUSE

In past century,

Women's were in cornered box

In their partithe cular duty

Of living without any rights

And not allowed to act as a unique lady.

The words of real poets

The lyrics of perfect singer

The dialogues of themeful director

The speech of excellent motivators

Awaken the women from the cornered box.

The word with full of optimism

Fires in every women's heart.

Some came forward

But most went backward

Many leaders fought for the freedom of women.

Intercession fighting for women

By honourable leaders

Never fed up in any case.

The energetic leaders,

Lost, lacked everything.

They had done not to get life for them

But to give life for every women

Who bend herself with

Fear, frustration, feeble.

This is how they got freedom.

At present century,

Women 's were breaking all the rules

What the conditions they were prohibited to do.

Not the rules to get disciplined

But the rules which drowns women.

Women of the world !

Weep not for any case,

Weary not for any downs,

Weak not when get sick,

In the ways of life.

Wake up from the ignorance

Awake the shoulders to raise,

Aware of the matters that you face,

Await for the success that you worked hard,

Make the nations to astonish at the women creature.

CAN OR CANNOT

Can or cannot justifies

Optimistic and pessimistic outcomes.

Closing up the glowing candle hides the light.

Opening up the glowing candle reveals the light.

Human (we) destined to

Be good and do good by God.

Lot's of six senses humane

Light up our candle on the candlestick

That might be seen by all.

Not too covered up with a bushel

That might be unseen by all.

So, induce other with the hop

You can, lest of you can't.

SELFLESS SACRIFICE

He came to the world

Not to live for himself,

But for myself

Wherever I am.

He is unknown to me

But, he knows me

To do something for him

Wherever I am.

I hate him

But he loves me

With the love of selfless

Wherever I am.

He shown his love not with wounding as a man

But by sacrificing his life

Until his last shed of blood and said "seek me"

Wherever I am.

In the hopeless world

I felt that he is my hope

Because, I experienced his love

Wherever I am.

He came to the world for me.

He loves me even i hate him.

Now, that 'He' is my God with me

Wherever I am.

UNDEFILED LOVE

I see you amidst

In the human creature

In school going stage.

I admired by your truthful smile

That made me drowsy.

Feel of true love, sense, integrity

In you I felt.

The happy which I experienced in you

That was not experienced before.

Your far relationship

Yield pain in me.

But far made me to

Be fair in love much more.

I loved, loving, will love

Until my soul sign the earth- “Goodbye”.

HOLLOWNESS

Long years after,

Longing alone in my path

Of cornered life.

I discern emptiness in me.

The comrade who was with me

Is not there with me.

Everything was abnormal

When i entered into mine

I found vacant

Expect my properties lone.

Empty place yearn hollowness

Hollowness holds my hand

Hand of senseless

Sense me to shed tears

Tears teared my memory of her

Memories remained me to throw everything

Everything remains silence

Silence remembered her

Her absence pursue me to feel of

Being alone.

PEACE MAKER

Love doesn't signifies in younger's stage

It signifies in every stage.

By expression of gesture and posture

Through the soul of every people

Love doesn't have jealous

But it have marvellous (thing).

Furious are prevailed by love

To unite every soul.

Love unites life

To eliminate the knife

Which produces rival

Between the life travel.

Love is the symbol

Of the humble

This need to be spread across the wall (world)

Of every people's mall(house).

BOW-WOW

Farmers bow to sow and reap

Readers bow to read the book to become scholars.

People bow to pray to receive blessings.

The word “bow” emphasizes humbleness.

When we bow before someone.

We receive the word wow from someone due to our bowness.

2

QUOTES

" Once I was searching my real
Companion
Now I were cheated because the real
Companion is was in me
Who I am"

" Speaking with the conscience is the best conversation of the individual in the world"

" More expected person
Will must be cheated,
Because they failed to accept the most reality".

" Don't pick up the role models from the higher
Observe the lower, that teaches you to be a role model".

" Worry not that you are at least,
Watch the beautiful butterfly that comes from the small warm.
Look, how precious we are?"

ȹȹȹ

" Handle every hard situation in silence is tough to apply,
But smart to handle in the process of silence."

ȹȹȹ

"Real love does not depend upon
The number of emotions.
But, it depends upon the
Quantity of eliminating wrong records".

ȹȹȹ

" Status doesn't bring life to live
But satisfaction brings status to live a happy life".

ȹȹȹ

" Pen is the speaker of voiceless people
Single pen can strike the mind of pessimistic into optimistic people".

ȹȹȹ

" Your tease on others
Will cease your growth".

ȹȹȹ

"Have trust in you
Spread the happiness to others
Be a healer of the woundedness".

ȹȹȹ

" Faith is the weapon to shackle the forthcoming persecutions"

ღღღ

" Love each other like yourself.
Because there was lack of love
Among family
Among friends
Among society.
Please consider love as biggest source to
Unite the society.
Love covers more sin".

ღღღ

"Every writer's thoughts and writings were hidden in their last page of the note".

ღღღ

" Every pain was hidden in the smile of a man who understands the life"

ღღღ

" If you want to eliminate expectations from your loved one's.
Learn to applicate acceptance of the person in your loved heart's."

ღღღ

"You may least in range ,
To help the poor
But, the man who help the poor in his least range ,
Will shame the man who have more".

ღღღ

"Select friend and change
If he is bad, change him.
That change bring the world into good change".

ÞÞÞ

"The wound which causes by accident will be cured
But the wound which causes by tongue will never be cured".

ÞÞÞ

"Subract the word I AM.
Add the word WE.
Multiply the word US.
To spread your thoughts".

ÞÞÞ

" Don't stop your desire by your words
Stop by your action towards it".

ÞÞÞ

"In the world, living things have humanity.
And non-living things don't have humanity.
But now it is reversity.
To change it, you people become a man of charity".

ÞÞÞ

"A heart which carries the love of god
Will not cheat anyone and cannot be cheated by anybody".

♡♡♡

"We know what God can do in our life
But, God knows what he should do in our life"

3

Little Thoughts to Live

LIFE (BI) CYCLE

Bicycle is a series of events that are regularly repeated in the same order. As like life is also repeated with same order. The main parts of the cycle are wheels, saddle, handle bars, two pedal, chain rings, bell and parking rack. The heart of the cycle is chain rings. Life is like a cycle and it has different parts. God has given a life cycle to each individual in the world. Same cycle but different brand. Brand is a unique of particular person and how we're journeying in our bicycle is very important. Saddle is the place which we used to sit, two handle bar depicts our of direction, two pedal are the hurdles where we come across by prevailing. The two handle bar is very useful for us to hold up in journey. Because, pedalling in equal force deviates the direction. Handle bar are use to take a very short break in journey. Bicycle parking rack is used to take rest and not to quit the journey. Cycle carrier signifies whom we're choosing to take part with them. The selecting of right person to sit behind our saddler in cycle carrier is most essential. It is like two hands which creates sound. As, the person who take part in carrier should one-minded of a person in saddler. If he jiggle, the journey rider cannot travel to his destined path. Two pedal are the hurdles which we prevail lest of getting tired. In this area, we should not see another person's cycle. That makes us to fell down in the midst of journey. As I have said before, Chain rings are the heart of bicycle. Yea, it's true. If chain rings gets loosed. It struck during our travel and we cannot continue any more. Remaining part, cycle bell-this is a foremost of journey and also in life to skip or asking others to get away from their path. We horn it due to our distraction. We are living in the busy world, even we don't have time to analyse our life process.

Let's learn from a simple transport "BICYCLE". And not of wasting time of searching to learn from high (beyond us) things or matter. Proverb says Go and learn from an ant. Simultaneously learn from a bicycle for cycling your life cheerfully.

TARRY UNTIL YOUR WISH COMES TRUE

If you tarry for a, bus you'll receive it, the job you'll achieve it, the food you'll swallow it, plan you'll succeed it, the prayer you'll get an answer and so on. These all will shower abundantly on you when you tarry for a thing. Being tarry/waiting gives us startled and hurry. Why we want to tarry? And why we mightn't get without tarry? The answer is, for each thing i.e., to get food deeds there's a particular period to obtain it. Let us look the God's creatures especially flowers. We get flowers from trees. But we can't see flowers always in the trees, because it has the period to sprout, to bud, to bloom and to wither. Actually we have a procedure through this blooming flowers. How beautiful it is to look on the procedure. When we keenly notice on this procedure we can learn something to live our life. The main thing is the tree is so lamboyant that we will shine(bloom) in its when it tarry. In the busy as a bee world, people dislike to tarry, this happens from childishness to second childishness. They couldn't tarry for preparing food. So, they are touching the button and within a hour, they touch their food. How it is? It is so fast and we can say many examples such as to pick bus , to purchase thing and so on. People are choosing their mask in day-today life as Oliver Goldsmith says in "The City Night Place". But let us analyse ourselves, stop running just have a pause in your track and tickle your mind where we should tarry. Most people failing to analyse their way. This short thought is for the readers as well as writer. How marvellous creatures we are, the entry of fault in our life is common and unusual.

But, the six sense "humane" of we should analyse our path. When we tarry we don't need to tremble in life only we have to be thankful for God. " Tarry, still your problems run in your track. And see your victory of being in your track". " Tarry, still your enemies laugh at you. And smile when your enemies see at you".

ANGUISH ECHO OF NEEDY

Once there was a family with mother, father, a girl child and Grandmother. Father was a drunkard man. He died with taking of extreme alcohol. In the absence of father, his wife also died with grief. Now, the family remains with the only child and her grandmother . The girl name was unknown, she was so little, a school-going child. There is no possession kept by her parents. Obviously, they are needy and not poor. Grandma is struggling a lot to take care of her. One day, there was no food, she cannot continue her study because of depression and hungry. The little, needy, voiceless small girl told her grandma " Patti, take the match stick box and take chemical powder of the top and mix in water and let us drink and die" No more to live with pain and misery. Some children will cry to their parents to buy what they do not need. As we also will be adamant to buy some things which we like. But this girl doesn't have the opportunity to be adamant to buy more and to ask with rights. This is real tale happened. What are the things we're doing to eliminate the voice of anguish. We only opening our voice widely to get more and more. We are not sophisticated with the properties. As a lion, we waiting to hunt something from the forest . Only one thing we should keep in our mind, nothing is permanent. We are born to live and we have death. We came to earth with naked and we'll go from the earth with naked. So, nothing is permanent. As I have said we are born to death; if we born surely we will face death. So what we are going to do with so, so and so much of earthly things. With our property, we should share with the needy people. Specially, there are people who word for the needy and make them to be well-settle. Even more are there without this hand.

"A man helping poor

Is giving debt to God"

A earning man saving his money in his hole pockets. Then how he can be happy. Those who have lot of money, properties and possession. They have disease and they cannot live peace and cheerful life. One of the drama in Tamil literature, "yawning Voice" distinguishes the joy of filthy and wealthy people.

"Give yours to others.

And others will give yours|"

Helping others will help you when you're in need. This activities make you happy. A man with lots of gold and money will make him grief and to watch over it always. So that he cannot be happy always. Philosophy doesn't says that you should purchase anything. But it says to keep and stock things what you need for today and don't worry for tomorrow. Because tomorrow is not in your hand. It is in the hand of creator. Throughout the World, Nation, State, District anguish voice are echoing. We should try to reply a small group need. When each one of us develop from small it unites big and change the World, Nation, State, District into a cheerful voice.

"Speaking to help others is lesser than acting it in reality".

TRUST

Trust is one of the traits of human being. Trust on people is difficult. Trust defines believing others for a matter. But those who believes only on people especially wrong people their life will tear into pieces. It takes time to rebuild. In one boundary, overwhelming of trust on others will give birth destruction. Particularly, a special book(Holy Book) quoth "Blessed are all they that put their trust in him".(Ps.2:12) You may have question about the above lines says that don't have trust beyond. But this verse of holy book "Blessed are all they that put their trust in him. So, who is him. "Him" is passive voice of "He". He points out the creator, maker of this world i.e., Lord, son of God and Holy spirit. We people living in this earth with people. How can't we trust in them. As a human we are dependent and we should trust others for a matters. For ex: a man should be dependent on Barbour to lock the hair, Cobbler to stitch sandals , shopkeepers to purchase. Whether it is possible not to dependent on people. Yes, we want to be dependent on others and trust others with confine. Don't keep human as in the place of God or not not cling unto them always.

"Honey is good.

But overdose of it gives bad"

My dear brothers and sisters, focus on God who is invisible with eyes but visible in our souls. Main part of the trust is in the time of trouble on God. Many of us fail to focus of God in the time of trouble and instead they started to orate a false report of God. The babble with many useless words because of their weariness in heart. The upright man Job, babbled to God in the period of his temptation. So, that in the last chapter God asked Job "Why you use the word with unnecessary things". Job beseeched God to forgive him and he prayed for his friend who spake against him.

So that God has turned away the captivity of Job and blessed him with twice of his past. “Trust him always in his waiting”. If God has refination in your life process. He quiets for a day, month, year. But we should be waiting for God and not for man to argue our miseries. Wait, Wait, Wait and it make us weight(not in Kg of body) before the less of enemy. We can’t trust God always because we are filled with carnal things. Ask help from God to keep and to put trust on him always even in the time of tribulation. Repeat yourself the word “Trust” it fold our arms and make us strong.

“Trust on good people

Trust on invisible

Trust on his waiting

Trust on him who gives ticket to heaven”.

Thank You

♡♡♡

Printed by Libri Plureos GmbH in Hamburg,
Germany